IN SEARCH OF CIGARETTE HOLDER MAN

Recent Doonesbury Books by G.B. Trudeau

Read My Lips, Make My Day, Eat Quiche and Die!
Give Those Nymphs Some Hooters!
You're Smokin' Now, Mr. Butts!
I'd Go With the Helmet, Ray
Welcome to Club Scud!
What Is It, Tink, Is Pan in Trouble?
Quality Time on Highway 1
Washed Out Bridges and Other Disasters

In Large Format

The Doonesbury Chronicles
Doonesbury's Greatest Hits
The People's Doonesbury
Doonesbury Dossier: The Reagan Years
Doonesbury Deluxe: Selected Glances Askance
Recycled Doonesbury: Second Thoughts on a Gilded Age
Action Figure!
The Portable Doonesbury

A DOONESBURY BOOK
by G. B. TRUDEAU

IN SEARCH OF CIGARETTE HOLDER MAN

ANDREWS and McMEEL   A UNIVERSAL PRESS SYNDICATE COMPANY   KANSAS CITY

———————— ATTENTION: SCHOOLS AND BUSINESSES ————————

Andrews and McMeel books are available at quantity discounts with bulk purchase for educational, business, or sales promotional use. For information, please write to: Special Sales Department, Andrews and McMeel, 4900 Main Street, Kansas City, Missouri 64112.

"If there were no conspiracy, the government would have had to invent one so that we would believe they are doing their work."

— DANIELA GARCIA, ON THE ASSASSINATION OF MEXICAN PRESIDENTIAL CANDIDATE LUIS COLOSIO

14

27

35

43

44

58

Panel 1:
HAS THE JURY REACHED A VERDICT?

WE HAVE, YOUR HONOR...

Panel 2:
WE FIND THE DEFENDANT GUILTY OF GIVING THE PLAINTIFF AN UNFAIR GRADE, THUS DEFAMING THE ENTIRE GRECO-AMERICAN ATHLETIC COMMUNITY. WE AWARD THE PLAINTIFF DAMAGES OF $5 MILLION.

Panel 3:
THE COURT THANKS THE JURY FOR ITS SERVICE...

Panel 4:
...DESPITE ITS MORONIC VERDICT.

HEY, WHAT DO YOU WANT FOR $12 A DAY?

Panel 5:
PETER, THE GUILTY VERDICT IS BEING HAILED TODAY BY A **VERY** HAPPY GRECO-AMERICAN ATHLETIC COMMUNITY...

Panel 6:
ALBERT SLOCUM, WHAT ARE YOUR FEELINGS RIGHT NOW? ARE YOU FEELING ANYTHING? YOU MUST HAVE SOME PRETTY AMAZING FEELINGS, SON!

Panel 7:
I DO, ROLAND, BUT I'LL TELL YOU, IT'S BEEN A LONG, DIFFICULT TRIAL. EVEN WITH THE $5 MILLION AWARD, WE NEED TIME TO HEAL.

Panel 8:
PARTY! PARTY!

YO! LET THE HEALING BEGIN!

Panel 9:

WE'RE TALKING TO WALTER BOOTH, JURY FOREMAN FOR THE DEADMAN TRIAL. MR. BOOTH, WHAT MADE THE DIFFERENCE FOR THIS JURY?

Panel 10:
WELL, I'D SAY THE PLAINTIFF'S SIDE DID A REAL GOOD JOB OF PERSUADING US THAT WALDEN COLLEGE HAD SOLD ITSELF AS A PLACE WHERE A KID COULD EXPECT STRAIGHT "A"s.

Panel 11:

ALSO, JURORS ARE HUMAN. THERE WASN'T ONE OF US WHO COULDN'T REMEMBER WHAT IT WAS LIKE TO RECEIVE A "B."

Panel 12:

NO KIDDING, MAN? YOU GOT "B"s, TOO?

WELL, IN OUR DAY, WE CALLED THEM "D"s.

Panel 1: OKAY. TOP OF PAGE 73, YOU'RE BEING INTERVIEWED BY F.B.I. AGENTS IN PORTLAND...

Panel 2: "NEITHER JEFF NOR I KNEW ANYTHING ABOUT THIS! WE WERE SHOCKED! HURTING NANCY WAS THE FURTHEST THING FROM OUR MINDS! WE'RE **COMPLETELY** INNOCENT!"

Panel 3: GOOD! NOW PICK IT UP AFTER AGENT #2'S SPEECH ABOUT HOW LYING TO THE F.B.I. IS A FEDERAL CRIME...

Panel 4: "I JUST REMEMBERED— JEFF DID IT!"
AND AGAIN! THIS IS A CAREER MOVE— **SELL** IT!

Panel 5: OKAY, MS. BOOPSTEIN, LET'S HAVE YOU READ JUST ONE MORE SPEECH — TONYA'S FAREWELL AT LILLEHAMMER. FROM THE TOP OF PAGE 117, PLEASE!

Panel 6: "SKATING IN THE OLYMPICS WAS ALWAYS MY DREAM. IT WAS THE DREAM THAT KEPT ME GOING. SKATING HERE WAS THAT DREAM'S FULFILLMENT..."

Panel 7: "THE DREAM OF GOING TO THE OLYMPICS IS OVER! IT IS A DREAM COME TRUE! NOW I HAVE A DIFFERENT DREAM, A SHINY, **NEW** DREAM...,"

Panel 8: "I DREAM OF... OF... NOT GOING TO JAIL!"
BIGGER! SHE'S **PUMPED!**

Panel 9: I DIDN'T GET THE TONYA ROLE, B.D.
YOU DIDN'T? HEY, SORRY, BABE...

Panel 10: WELL, I SUPPOSE IT'S JUST AS WELL. IT WOULD HAVE BEEN A VERY TOUGH ROLE TO GET A HANDLE ON.
WHAT DO YOU MEAN?

Panel 11: WELL, TONYA'S THIS AMBITIOUS, YOUNG WANNABE, DRIVEN BY DREAMS OF STARDOM, AND MARRIED TO AN ABUSIVE LUNKHEAD WHO TRIES TO RUN HER LIFE.

Panel 12: I JUST COULDN'T RELATE.
YEAH, SOUNDS LIKE A STRETCH.

70

OLLIE RESPONDS TO THE GIPPER.
FRIENDS, AS YOU MAY HAVE HEARD, MR. REAGAN HAS RECENTLY ACCUSED ME OF LYING ABOUT HIS ROLE IN IRANGATE...
BOOO!
HEY, HEY! NONE OF THAT! RONALD REAGAN WAS THE GREATEST PRESIDENT OF THIS CENTURY!
REMEMBER, FRIENDS, MR. REAGAN IS 83 YEARS OLD! OF COURSE HIS MEMORY ISN'T WHAT IT ONCE WAS! WE MUST BE UNDERSTANDING OF HIS MENTAL LAPSES, NOT CONDEMNING!
CUE MISTING EYES.
AFTER ALL, THIS COUNTRY WAS BUILT BY THE FORMERLY YOUNG...
©B Trudeau

OLLIE'S CAMPAIGN VEHICLE RETURNS FROM THE RALLY...
FOX ONE, WE'RE HEADED FOR HOME BASE!
DUKE, I JUST DON'T UNDERSTAND HOW REAGAN COULD BETRAY ME...
WE WERE SO CLOSE! DURING OUR PRIVATE MEETINGS, HE USED TO TELL ME I WAS THE CAN-DO SON HE NEVER HAD!
IT WASN'T UNTIL AFTER THE HEARINGS THAT I FOUND OUT HE ALREADY HAD A COUPLE OF SONS! HE'D MISLED ME—AGAIN!
CUE CATCH IN THROAT.
BUT I... I FORGAVE HIM. I SOLDIERED ON!
©B Trudeau

LISTEN TO THIS, DUKE: "WILL DOUG WILDER REJOIN THE RACE FOR SENATOR OF VIRGINIA? IF SO, HE POSES A MAJOR NEW THREAT TO FORMER IRANGATE CONSPIRATOR OLIVER L. NORTH!"
MAY I SEE THAT, COLONEL?
HELP YOURSELF.
PERMISSION TO SECURE THE PERIMETER, SIR.
NAH, HE'S OLD AND SLOW. I CAN TAKE HIM.
©B Trudeau

Panel 1: SIR, IT LOOKS LIKE YOU'RE FINALLY CATCHING A BREAK ON THE UPCOMING WHITEWATER HEARINGS...

Panel 2: HOW'S THAT? / WELL, IT'S FINALLY DAWNED ON THE REPUBLICANS THAT THEY'RE GOING TO HAVE TO PRODUCE AN ACTUAL SCANDAL FOR THE HEARINGS...

Panel 3: DOLE AND THE G.O.P. LEADERSHIP ARE NOW SCRAMBLING TO PATCH TOGETHER A STRATEGY THAT WON'T COMPLETELY EMBARRASS THEM.

Panel 4: ...AND THEN WE WAIT FOR A WITNESS TO BLURT SOMETHING OUT. / BOB, DEAR, IS THERE A PLAN B?

Panel 5: SENATOR DOLE ASSEMBLES HIS WHITEWATER TROOPS. / OKAY, REALITY CHECK: WHY ARE WE HOLDING NATIONALLY TELEVISED HEARINGS? WHAT ARE THEY ACTUALLY ABOUT?

Panel 6: THE HEARINGS ARE ABOUT AN INVESTMENT MADE 15 YEARS AGO, AND WHETHER THE CLINTONS DID ANYTHING IMPROPER WHILE LOSING MONEY ON IT.

Panel 8: THANK GOD FOR THE COVER-UP. / BINGO. THAT'S OUR FOCUS.

Panel 9: THE G.O.P. LEADERSHIP IS BRAINSTORMING WHITEWATER. / IF I MAY, BOB, DEAR? / THE CHAIR RECOGNIZES CONGRESSWOMAN DAVENPORT.

Panel 10: I THINK WE SHOULD TREAD CAREFULLY WITH THESE HEARINGS. IF THERE IS, IN FACT, MALFEASANCE, THEN BY ALL MEANS, WE SHOULD BRING IT TO LIGHT!

Panel 11: BUT IF THERE'S NO REAL SCANDAL AT THE CENTER OF WHITEWATER, THIS ALL COULD BACKFIRE. WE SHOULD ASK OURSELVES HONESTLY: WHY ARE WE DOING THIS?

Panel 12: BECAUSE IT'S **PAYBACK TIME**, BABY! / THE CHAIR RECOGNIZES SENATOR D'AMATO.

82

91

...AND I THINK THE RECORD THAT IS MINE WILL SHOW THAT I WAS A **VERY** EFFECTIVE VICE PRESIDENT, A **MAJOR** PLAYER IN THE ADMINISTRATION!

...UNLIKE **CHENEY** OR **KEMP** OR **BAKER**, GUYS WHO MISMANAGED **EVERYTHING**, CAUSED THAT '92 TRAIN WRECK!

BUT, MR. Q, YOU WERE HALF THE TICKET—DON'T YOU BEAR SOME RESPONSIBILITY?

GET REAL. I WAS ONLY VEEP. THE JOB'S A JOKE.

OH, RIGHT.

MR. Q., NOT TO BE CRUEL, BUT IF PEOPLE IN THIS COUNTRY AGREE ON ANYTHING, IT'S THAT YOU'RE NOT PRESIDENTIAL MATERIAL...

DOESN'T THIS RUN AT THE PRESIDENCY MEAN YOU'RE IN THE DEEPEST KIND OF DENIAL?

NOT AT ALL!

IT MEANS THE PARTY'S IN TERRIBLE SHAPE! IT MEANS ALL THE OTHER POTENTIAL GOP CANDIDATES ARE **LOSERS** OR **HAS-BEENS**!

POINT TAKEN. YOU GOT ME THERE.

HEE, HEE! THANKS. HOW SWEET IT IS!

SEE, MARK, I WOULDN'T EVEN **HAVE** TO TEST THE WAUGHTERS IF IT WEREN'T FOR THIS MEDIA CARICATURE YOU GUYS CREATED! ALL THE JOKES HAVE BEEN **COMPLETELY** UNFAIR!

WELL, SIR, THE FACT IS THAT JOKES DON'T WORK IF THE AUDIENCE CAN'T PERCEIVE THE TRUTH BEHIND THEM...

YOU'VE HAD A **LOT** OF MEDIA EXPOSURE, SIR. ISN'T IT POSSIBLE THE PUBLIC FORMED ITS UNFAVORABLE IMPRESSION OF YOU ALL ON ITS **OWN**?

LET ME THINK ABOUT THAT... OKAY, FINISHED! WHAT NOW?

ALL DONE. THANKS FOR COMING BY.